Fic KAV   c.1

Kavanaugh, James J.

A fable /

A
FABLE

James Kavanaugh

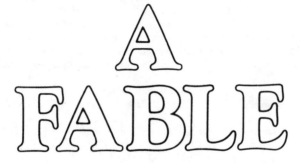

A FABLE

Illustrations by Daniel Biamonte

E. P. DUTTON   •   NEW YORK

For information contact:
Elsevier-Dutton Publishing Co., Inc., 2 Park Avenue, New York, N.Y. 10016

Library of Congress Catalog Card Number: 80-66799

ISBN: 0-525-93154-6

Published simultaneously in Canada by
Clarke, Irwin & Company Limited, Toronto and Vancouver

Designed by Nicola Mazzella

10 9 8 7 6 5 4 3 2 1

First Edition

To those:
    Who still believe
        In a village called Harmony.

Especially to those:
    Who are determined
        To live there.

JAMES KAVANAUGH
Nevada City, California

CHAPTER ONE

Once upon a time in the foothills of a great mountain range, there was a peaceful village called Harmony. Its colorful frame houses rolled across a fresh green valley and crawled halfway up the surrounding hills. Beyond the hills, to the north and east, were the towering peaks and bluffs of the Explorer Mountains, standing like brown and purple giants suspended from the heavens and crowned with snow from late September till the middle of summer. Each year in spring, boiling rivulets of melting snow splashed down the highest mountains, gouging out streams that flowed swollen and frothy into the Singing River. The river then roared through the foothills and across rich green meadows, tearing fiercely at banks of marsh grass and wild flowers until it reached Harmony. There it more leisurely spread out and wound its way southerly through the village, then picked up speed as it narrowed and turned west and rushed impatiently to the sea in an unending circle of life.

Harmony had remained a world unto itself since to travel there was arduous enough to be almost impossible. According to an ancient edict, reinforced by centuries of tradition, strangers were not welcome lest they introduce novel attitudes that might infect a tranquil way of life. For the same reason, no one who left was permitted to return. As was said in a well-known adage, "It is not kindness to offer the fox a bed among the hens."

Actually there was little reason to leave Harmony, for it was as beautiful and fruitful a place as there was in the whole world. There was a rich, fertile soil combed carefully from the earth and deposited by the retreating waters of a river that eons ago had flowed through the entire valley. Everywhere were towering pines and whispering cypresses, at times gathered in silent reflective forests, or scattered among live oaks and elms and maples like invincible sentries that stared beyond the mountains to protect the

village. And scattered about the hills like stone monuments were massive granite boulders, tossed there like pebbles by powerful glacial arms thousands of decades before. Hidden in the hills were mirrored lakes sculpted from rock by the fists of an ancient ice flow that resisted all containment.

Deer grazed on tender leaves of wild plants and fruit trees and crept cautiously at twilight to sip at the dark pools of the Singing River. Bobcats and raccoons prowled the groves at night, black bears munched blueberries and strawberries at the rim of the nearest hill, porcupines and opossums lurked in the brush, silver and gold trout flashed behind rocks or waited along the banks of the river to surprise a caddis or may fly. Occasionally a grinning red fox was seen crossing a dirt road, and silver wolves sang love songs to a distant mate under a full moon. Mallards and widgeons nibbled in silent swamps or played on quiet ponds of water lilies, ring-necked pheasants and quail waddled along vineyards or in cornfields, and in the fall the Canadian geese and dazzling white swans flew in perfect formation from the wheat fields to sleep along the edge of the river.

As the village grew through countless generations, houses of stone and wood had moved from the edge of the river up the slopes of the hills in neat rows of red and yellow, blue and brown and lavender. Each house had its own small garden, a neatly stacked woodpile, a few cows and goats, chickens and pigs, and a large fieldstone chimney with wisps of white smoke rising above the distant mountain peaks to join the floating clouds. In the center of the village was the town hall and a giant stone church with a large bell tower and stained glass windows much older than anyone alive. Across from the church was the square, a large park with rows of flowers and a waterfall, a wooden bridge across the Singing River, and benches along a cobblestone walk. In the center of the square was an elevated stage for summer concerts and plays.

Each newborn child was given a celebration with wine and dancing in the square and the ringing of church bells across the valley. Each death was a quiet period of mourning with a solemn eulogy in the stone church and the echoing faith of the congregation chanting its plaintive hymns to the faraway mountains that touched the heavens. A marriage was a weekend pageant with games and music, mounds of fresh bread and simmering stews, green vegetables and steaming potatoes, fresh apple pies and straw-berry tarts, red wine and thick cider, and dancing and singing far into the night.

There was a hospital of white stone and airy, bright rooms at the edge of the village in a grove of walnut trees. On the opposite side was a wooden school bordering a pine forest. And behind the church was a well-kept graveyard. There was no jail or bank or orphanage, no police or soldiers or newspaper. Crime was rare and was dealt with by families themselves, or by the mayor and village council. Punishment was most often hard work and restriction from celebrations, and, most of all, the shame of the community. Elections were held every five years and the candidates for mayor or the village council were elected by a shout of approbation in the square. The elders, that is, the aged and respected citizens, took turns conducting Sunday services in the church, telling simple, traditional stories and parables from the archives of Harmony, offering brief prayers of thanks to God, and selecting songs that even the oldest and youngest knew by heart. After the service there was fresh bread and fruit, milk and cheese for everyone in the square. The men lingered to talk of their work, the women laughed and fondled babies, then hurried home to prepare dinner, the children chased and shouted until it was time to leave.

There was work enough for everyone and each took it for granted that hard work was a basic part of life. The individual craftsmanship of each family, honed through centuries of tradition, was a source of great personal pride. The tailor made beautiful clothes for the cobbler and miller in return for perfectly stitched shoes and the best flour. The weaver exchanged smooth cloth for fat strawberries or a fine feathered hat. The carpenter and woodsman were as respected as the miller and blacksmith, the housewife as important as the healer or mayor. Only the elders, men and women too old or feeble to labor, were exempted from work and afforded a special respect and dignity earned from the gathered wisdom and dedication of a long life. A gifted musician or storyteller, a talented painter or singer was considered a special treasure from God for the joy of the whole community. But, no matter what work was done, it was taken for granted that it would be done well. A common saying, often quoted by an elder on Sunday, maintained:

To make a good candle is to honor the bee and one's self.

Another adage said:

Imperfect work is an insult to the clouds that labor to cool the meadow.

Through the years there was little reason in Harmony for greed or jealousy or unresolved strife, and when any of these problems emerged, the elders offered words of comfort and understanding, insisting that the whole village belonged to everyone and everyone belonged to the whole village. Of course there were disagreements, even tragedies, but they concerned all the people. As was said:

A single unsettled stone can create an avalanche.

When a young tinsmith drowned, or the tanner lost two children in a landslide, everyone was upset. The entire village mourned a boy born without sight, a young girl with a twisted, deformed body, a grandmother who lost her wits, or a fierce quarrel between two brothers over a piece of their father's land. On such occasions all of Harmony seemed distressed until the bereaved were comforted or enemies made lasting peace. Quarrels were not allowed to smolder without confrontation and discussion, the witless and crippled were cared for at home and protected by the populace, and grief was shared in a multitude of hearts and compassionate spirits.

For the most part the people of Harmony were strong of body and will. Discipline was learned from the earliest years, respect for elders was imbibed almost at nursing, and forgiveness and understanding and brotherly love were as obvious as the mountains respecting the boundaries of the meadows and rivers. An ancient story was told by one of the elders each year at the planting celebration on a Sunday in mid-April. It was always told the same way.

Once a man was thirsting at the bottom of a high hill. His eyes saw the deer gathering at the brow of the hill to drink and his ears heard the splashing of water. At the bidding of his eyes and ears the man began to climb, but his feet objected: "Why must we obey the eyes and ears and work so hard? The knees do nothing!" So he began to walk on his knees. Soon the knees complained: "What of the hands?" Immediately he began walking on his hands, but the hands pointed out the futility of the climb since only the mouth wanted water. Finally the man collapsed and died on the hill. We, all of us, are that man and each part depends on the whole. No one is greater or less, no one is sufficient to himself. Thus says our ancient wisdom.

One Sunday morning during the harvest celebration, when the villagers gathered in the square for breakfast, there was a shout of confusion and surprise at the far edge of the park by the walnut grove. Two of the elders who had been chatting nearby made their way to the circle of bewilderment and saw a strange young man lying on the ground. The boys and girls parted at the approach of the old men. The stranger, pale and exhausted, looked up at them weakly. The children held their breath in excitement.

"Who are you and whence have you come?" one of the elders asked gently.

"I am Oudeis," he said quietly. "I come from far across the mountains."

"You are hungry." The elder signalled a boy and girl to bring bread and goat's milk.

The stranger ate and drank almost voraciously. A crowd began to gather and the tailor noticed the stranger's torn cloak.

"I will bring him something fine to wear."

The elder nodded agreement. The cobbler approached and went off to bring leather sandals. Then the elder bade Oudeis to follow him and took him to his own home, prepared water for his bath, and offered him his own bed on which to rest. That night the elder and his wife slept on the floor by the stone fireplace. In the morning his wife prepared a hearty breakfast of bread, eggs, fruit, and warm milk, while the elder walked to the healer's house and led him back to observe the stranger.

"Is he well enough to travel?"

The healer briefly examined Oudeis. "Quite sound," he said.

The elder looked at the stranger kindly. "We are all grateful that you survived your difficult journey. Now we must ask you to rest for a few days and then return to your own people. We will prepare food for

your journey and two of our strongest young men will accompany you to the top of the distant mountains. From there it will be easy to find your own village."

"I am a townsman!" Oudeis exclaimed. "I do not want to return. There is no love where I live, only greed and indifference. Each man and woman is in a private war with every other. The rich amass what they can and the poor brood to divest them or plot dishonest ways to amass fortunes. No one is at peace in Prosperity. Even men of religion are as narrow and self-centered as the townspeople they serve. Men who do not work are rewarded and women seek to supplant men. The children are undisciplined and rude; the young, avaricious and ambitious only to succeed without effort. Families are without authority and understanding." The elder could hardly believe the words he was hearing but permitted Oudeis to continue.

"The old are ignored and neglected in Prosperity, the poor are despised and grudgingly placed on public doles, the sick are considered a burden and responsible for their own undoing. Only wealth and pleasure and physical health are thought to be of value. All of the old laws and traditions are mocked, politics has replaced justice, and new leaders make prisoners of their helpless disciples with strange, inhuman cults until the whole land seems to have grown mad. No one trusts anyone, a man's word means nothing, and lawyers are invoked at the slightest provocation, only to be confronted with other lawyers as evil as they are."

"What are lawyers?" the elder asked.

Oudeis paused. "Well, they are men and women who represent a person, advocates who speak for someone who seeks justice."

"Why do not men and women speak for themselves?"

"They find it difficult since the laws and court procedures are complex and confusing."

"Why not simplify the laws so that even children can understand? Justice is complex only when men and women are not honest."

Oudeis smiled patronizingly, "Life is not as simple in a large town. It is no longer easy to know what is right and wrong."

The elder spoke softly, "Size means nothing. A single family knows only chaos without truth and strong, honest leadership. You must return to your town and learn to be honest."

"What good is honesty if no one is honest?"

The elder paused. The question had never presented itself and he seemed puzzled.

"I am not sure," he said quietly.

Oudeis pleaded with him. "Please let me stay here that I too may learn to be honest!"

The elder was moved. "It is not my decision. I will request a meeting of the mayor and the council and all the elders. Perhaps the whole village must be present to decide in such a grave and unprecedented matter. We have never admitted a stranger to our village. Our ancient wisdom says: 'A single locust can destroy the entire harvest.' But you plead your case well and deserve a hearing."

After some preparation the elder arranged the meeting and addressed the stranger. "The whole village will gather in the church. The meeting will take place when all are assembled."

He had hardly spoken when the church bell began tolling and men and women and children filed from the shops and fields, from homes and school to take their places in church. Only the infirm were not expected to attend. When all were gathered in the oak benches, the mayor and council assembled on one side of the sanctuary, and the elders on the opposite side. Oudeis sat on a comfortable chair close to the congregation. An elder, white-headed and gentle, rose and spoke kindly.

"We are all aware of the stranger in our midst. We have not gathered here to harass or embarrass, certainly not to accuse, but Oudeis has requested to remain in our village because his own town has become an unhappy place without peace or honesty."

The congregation groaned spontaneously in shock and surprise, but were silent again when the hoary old man gently lifted a dark wrinkled hand.

"We know that his request is contrary to our ancient traditions: 'The quail does not warm the pigeon in winter.' But the same traditions teach that every reasonable request must receive a hearing: 'Even the crow sings if you understand his music.' For this reason we have called a meeting."

He addressed the stranger. "Oudeis, what work would you perform if you were to remain with us in the village of Harmony?"

"I am not really skilled at anything." He spoke haltingly.

There was an uncomfortable stirring among the villagers and another brief gasp of surprise. The elder again raised his hand softly.

"But surely you worked in Prosperity each day. Did you fell trees or plant them, bake bread or grind wheat or forge metal? What is your family's craft?"

"I did none of those things, and my family has no craft. Things do not work like that in Prosperity, but I have done very well. I have acquired a great deal of land and property."

Puzzlement erupted in the congregation and another elder spoke out. "How did you acquire more land and property than you need?"

Oudeis smiled at the naïveté. "I bought other people's land and sold it for profit."

"Why do parents not give their land to their children as we do? Our wisdom says, 'The sun warms the entire land and shares its heat with men and beasts and birds.' Is it not the same with the people of Prosperity?"

"No, it is not the same. In my town land is sold like meat and flour and cloth. Some people own much land and others want more, so they

23

buy it and sell it like apples to make a profit. And the land grows more valuable with every sale."

The people were shocked and a councilman interjected, "Why does anyone want more land than he can work on and enjoy?"

"In Prosperity a man can make money from all the things he owns. The more he owns, the more money he has and the more land and houses he can buy."

"What is money?" the mayor asked.

"Gold and silver, valuable metals that men and women in Prosperity prize. They are a means of exchange in our town. If I want a new cloak or more land, I give the seller the gold that he asks for whatever I buy."

The people were astounded and an elder asked, "But why are these metals so valuable? They cannot be eaten or drunk, they are not seeds that can be planted."

The people laughed loudly until Oudeis continued. "These metals are rare and precious, and people treasure them."

The congregation shook their heads in astonishment and the mayor, still confused, continued the questioning. "But how does the value of land

24

increase as you have said? It is always the same land."

"The price of everything increases when it is hard to get: meat, bread, flax. The land is no different."

"But surely there is land for everyone? The land belongs to all the people, and our possession of it is only a stewardship and a protection for one's family. No one can amass more than can be lived on or worked to be made fruitful."

Oudeis' head was weary. "I do not think I can explain it, but some people have much land and others have none."

The people were totally bewildered.

"And you made a living by buying another's land?"

"Yes."

"Did you plant trees or corn, remove rocks, or build a house?"

"No, I did none of those things. I only sold the house that another had built or the land that another had improved."

"Then you did nothing," said an elder, more in shock than in accusation. "No wonder there is no peace in Prosperity, and you are searching for honesty."

The people of Harmony continued to shake their heads. A tall, thin councilman spoke out, "But how can you stay here when you do not know how to work? We have no land to sell."

"I have gold, rather a great deal of it." Oudeis pointed to a leather purse he carried.

"Gold means nothing to us," the elder said. "Only your labor and craft purchases anything in Harmony. Can you dig a well or build a home for children?"

"Perhaps I could learn . . ."

"But you are already old enough."

"I know I can work hard," Oudeis pleaded. "It is beautiful here, the people are good, and I long to remain with you."

There was utter silence in the church. After what seemed several minutes, the elder who had opened the meeting spoke softly. "We will decide now."

The elders left the sanctuary through a rear door and were joined by the mayor and the council in a private meeting room. They returned in fifteen minutes. The spokesman stood next to Oudeis' chair and addressed the people.

"Our decision is a difficult one. This has never happened before in our history, but we have decided on the basis of what has been handed down. It seems unlikely that Oudeis can make it across the mountains because the snows will come early this year. Even the deer have already left the heights, and his journey could soon be hazardous, perhaps impossible. There is no reason to take such a risk. We will permit Oudeis to live among us until the summer when we will make a final decision."

Then the elder led the people in song and the meeting ended.

CHAPTER TWO

The next few weeks, Oudeis knew happiness for the first time in years. He lived with one of the elders and his wife who had an extra room. They treated him as their own beloved son and first taught him about gardening and the care of the livestock.

"When the spring returns, you will have your own small plot of land."

During the fall Oudeis was apprenticed to the potter, but soon proved too clumsy to mold the clay into the assorted shapes of bowls and plates. Small children already knew the secrets of glazing and firing, and it embarrassed him to be an awkward beginner. He tried furnituremaking and carpentry with equal lack of success and complained to the elder of the long hours of hard work.

"It is too difficult here. I am not accustomed to such hard work."

"Work is hard only when it is not suited to your own abilities. You must be patient and find what you do well. As has been said: 'Until the hidden spring breaks through the ground and bubbles free, the stream cannot flow.' You are still seeping painfully through limestone to reach the surface. It will be different when you finally feel the sun."

Oudeis protested, "There is nothing to do here except work. It gets boring."

"You are bored only because you are not yet ready to move in harmony with the seasons. Your eyes see but do not understand, your ears hear but do not comprehend. Too many sights and sounds lead to confusion and destroy energy. You must be still to hear the song of the hummingbird. Anyone who does not love the work he does can never be happy. 'The beaver does not hire the hare to build his dam, nor does the sheep perish because he gives up his wool.' "

"Is life only work?"

"Of course not. Life is creation and growth, death and rebirth, rest and return. Even the earth dies in winter, but only to await the explosion of spring. Perhaps when you only gathered gold, you lost the rhythm you share with stars and flowers. Your hands were screaming to plant or harvest, and you ignored them. How can your body remain strong when it does not do what it was meant to do? In Harmony even the oldest of the elders or the smallest child grows something, if only a few flowers. Not to grow something is to despise the earth."

Finally Oudeis began to work with the blacksmith, forging iron from ore mined in the nearby Red Mountain into simple farm tools and wagon wheels. It was hot, hard work that required great strength younger boys didn't have, and he gradually took some pride in his rudimentary abilities. He graduated from unloading the ore from wooden wagons to fanning the flame and stoking the clay furnace with charcoal that gave the iron the strength of crude steel. When he was finally skilled enough to extract the glowing ball of iron from the fire, then hammer it vigorously to expel the slag, and finally to work it into a coherent mass to be shaped and formed into a simple plow, he was ecstatic. It was the first time in his life that he had created anything. He asked the blacksmith endless questions about each step in the process and learned more quickly than the younger apprentices who had grown up watching the blacksmith at work and took it for granted that they would one day do what he did.

The blacksmith, a tall, reserved man of forty winters, spoke only when necessary. He grew increasingly fond of the exuberant Oudeis who learned so enthusiastically that he hated to end the day. At the approach of his first winter in the valley, it was decided that Oudeis should move in with the blacksmith and his wife and their three teenaged children, a dark-haired girl of seventeen winters with ruddy cheeks and brown laughing eyes and two strong boys of sixteen and fourteen winters.

The whole family loved Oudeis and enjoyed the stories he told of Prosperity where there were tall buildings of stone and paved streets, viands of every description and elegant ladies in fine furs with diamonds and rubies set in shining gold.

One night after a hearty meal of warm bread and lamb stew, the blacksmith's family settled before the open hearth of the stone fireplace and listened to more tales of the exciting town far across the mountains.

When Oudeis talked again of wealthy ladies wearing rings and bracelets of pure gold, the dark-haired daughter named Raven asked Oudeis if they might see the gold he stored in his leather purse. When he returned from his room and emptied out the gleaming yellow coins and nuggets, there was hardly a sound in the room. The boys stared open-mouthed, Raven's eyes gleamed like stars, and even the blacksmith and his gentle wife were speechless. Finally the blacksmith broke the silence, "I doubt it will grow any flowers."

They all laughed loudly and prepared to play cards by the fire while Oudeis gathered up his gold and stored it away in the drawer next to his feather bed.

The following week Oudeis addressed the blacksmith during a walk through the square after lunch and made a simple request.

"I would like to make a gold ring for Raven," he said.

"She has no need of it," said her father.

"I know that, but I would like to make a gift of it to her. It would make me happier than I know." He did not dare to say he loved her.

The blacksmith had grown to love Oudeis and found it hard to refuse him such a harmless request.

"Perhaps I should not interfere with your gift. A few months ago you did not have the knowledge to make anything. I can well understand that it will be as much a gift to you as to my dark-haired Raven. I give my permission."

Oudeis was overjoyed and rushed home to select a large nugget of purest gold, then raced back to the blacksmith shop to melt it down, shape it, and mold it until it was just right for Raven. By playing a silly game that same night he was able to measure the size of her finger and the following day he gave final shape to her gift.

"It is a beautiful work of art," the blacksmith said. "I am proud of what you have accomplished."

After the evening meal, when all were gathered in front of the fire, Oudeis withdrew the ring from his pocket and without a word slipped it on Raven's finger. Raven's eyes glowed excitedly.

"What is it?" she asked.

"A ring of gold I made for you."

"What is it for?"

"Just for you to wear. It announces how beautiful you are."

Her brothers laughed and made simple fun, the blacksmith and his gentle wife smiled proudly. Raven could not stop staring at it and kissed Oudeis warmly on the cheek.

"How can I thank you?"

"I should thank you. The gold never looked as beautiful before."

Soon the gold ring was the talk of the village and Raven was stopped a dozen times a day so that villagers could admire the gold ring Oudeis had made for her. The cobbler's wife, a gracious, golden-haired woman of great beauty, especially admired the ring and dreamed of it one night. At breakfast she admitted to her husband that she wanted one like it. The cobbler approached Oudeis the same day and asked him if he could make a similar ring for his beautiful wife. Oudeis hesitated.

"It was a special gift for Raven."

"I will make you a fine pair of shoes, the finest in all of Harmony if only you will make another ring."

"You do not understand," said Oudeis. "It was something personal I did for Raven. Besides, a gold ring is far more valuable than the finest pair of shoes, more than a dozen pair of shoes."

The cobbler was not put off. "I will give you a fine horse, my own favorite bay, a cloak of the finest cloth, and a feathered hat in addition to the leather shoes."

Oudeis hesitated. A bargaining sense which had grown dormant suddenly revived.

"How about a fine bow, five arrows, and a new leather apron, too?"

"Agreed," said the cobbler. And Oudeis made the ring.

It was only a few days before the carpenter's wife wanted a ring as well. Oudeis agreed if the carpenter would build a small barn for the horse on a piece of land he had set aside for his son. It was a choice parcel in the middle of the hill above the carpenter's house.

Reluctantly the carpenter assented. "My son is only nine," he said. "There will be another place for him when he is old enough to marry."

Soon the mason and the woodsman approached Oudeis and agreed to build him a house of stone and wood above the barn if he would make rings for their wives and daughters.

"A larger home than your own?" Oudeis asked.

"Larger than either of ours," said the mason. The woodsman nodded consent.

Soon Oudeis had a thriving business and lost interest in forging iron and making shovels. A gold bracelet he made for the healer's wife created a new sensation and soon Oudeis had furniture for his own house, livestock, an abundance of flour and canned fruit and vegetables, a towering wood-pile, and a fine assortment of tailored clothes. He had never been happier, riding his horse through the village in his red cloak and feathered gold hat and accepting the smiles and warm greetings of an admiring populace. Only the elders, the blacksmith's family, and a few more seemed saddened by it all. Especially Raven who seldom saw him anymore. Neither did she wear her ring.

"Something is wrong with all of this," said the blacksmith to his wife. She agreed.

The elders were almost silent since they did not know what to say.

"Soon there will be no more gold," said one of them. "Then Harmony will be as it was before."

Before long Oudeis realized that there were only a few gold coins and nuggets left in his purse and he feared an end to his good fortune. At first he raised the price of a gold ring beyond all limits, but even so, the mayor's wife insisted on having one, as if there were no price too great to pay. Oudeis enlarged his house, built a stone cellar and filled it with the finest wines, accumulated more clothes and livestock, and built another barn. Soon he was the richest man in all of Harmony but he knew he must have more gold to insure his place of honor in the village. He recalled the summers in Prosperity when he had panned for flakes of gold in mountain streams with his uncle.

One spring day he addressed the miner who was waiting to unload his wagon of ore outside the blacksmith's shop. "I would like to ride my horse and accompany you to the Red Mountain tomorrow when you go to gather iron ore," he said.

"It is a difficult journey," said the miner. "Although the heavy snow is only on the distant Explorer Mountains, the land is heavy with water and the Singing River is dangerously swollen and difficult to cross."

"My horse is strong," said Oudeis eagerly. "I will meet you early in the morning." He felt a strange excitement.

Each day after that, Oudeis accompanied the miner and his son to the Red Mountain. While they were digging the ore and carrying it across the river into the wagon, Oudeis explored an ancient riverbed and gravel promontories for traces of gold. One day, after a week of searching, his effort was rewarded. He found a large gold nugget lodged in a crevice near the bank of the Singing River. The following day he gathered loose gravel nearby and rotated it carefully in a shallow pan which he had dipped gently into the water. After a few minutes of sifting he saw abundant flakes of gold in the black residue and knew that the area was rich in deposits. He returned home without mentioning a word about his discovery and that night dreamed he had found a vast cavern of the purest gold.

The following days, he rode off with the miner and his son and vigorously panned for gold. He found four more small nuggets at bedrock

and filled a small leather pouch with the bright gold flakes. He said nothing of his success to anyone and made two more bracelets for additional livestock, fine-carved furniture, and four young servants, the children of his clients, to attend his every need. The servants were a novelty since no one in Harmony had ever worked outside his own home or the trade of his own family. Before long the mayor and the healer had servants as well. The elders were aghast and cited an ancient saying:

To yoke a man or woman like an ox or ass is to defile the ground and make the stars ashamed.

But no matter what the elders said, no one seemed to listen.

For the first time, strident arguments were more common in the square than friendly conversation and song. The miller refused a pair of shoes for a sack of fine flour and demanded a leather purse as well. The potter and woodsman quarreled over the value of logs, and the tanner doubled the price of his leather. Soon the quality of work and material diminished, and housewives complained that the flour was too coarse for fine bread. The cobbler made three grades of shoes, and the mason and woodsman traded inferior products. Only a few, like the blacksmith and the miner, were saddened by the transformation, but soon all had to work longer hours to afford what had once been taken for granted.

The elders seemed despondent when theft and drunkenness became common, and bands of young men and women gathered at night in the square to pass the time away from their families. It was as if parents had lost their authority, and a pestilence had taken possession of numerous hearts. The elders rang the church bells for a special meeting of the council and less than half of the village attended. Despite the poor attendance, the most eloquent of the elders addressed the assembly in a strong confident voice.

"Madness has come to our village and a dark cloud has settled over the Explorer Mountains. There is quarreling and discontent, and a greed we have never known before. Men and women ignore the beauty of the spirit and pay homage to trinkets of gold. Already there are factions of discontent and soon there will be war. We must take some action or 'The viper will swallow the mouse who is made sleepy by his strange movements.' We must act soon!"

A woman spoke firmly, "The stranger Oudeis must be sent away. He lords it over the people and seduces them with his gold. My own children would rather have gold than to learn the trade of their father."

"It is too late to send Oudeis away," said the blacksmith. "The whole village has been infected. We must fight back."

"But how?" asked the elder quietly.

The miner stood up to address the assembly. "The blacksmith and I have been talking," he said hesitantly. "Perhaps what we have to offer makes no sense, but these are critical times and we must do something."

He paused as if the unaccustomed public speech had tired him. He took a deep breath. "The gold which Oudeis introduced seems to be the destructive potion . . ."

"It should be gathered up and thrown away," said a thin, middle-aged woman almost in tears.

"That would only make the dissension greater," said the blacksmith. "As has been written, 'To blow on a spark could engulf the forest with fire.' "

The crowd grew quiet again and the miner continued. "What if there were an abundance of gold? Vast wagonloads of it."

"Is that possible?" asked the elder.

"What if it were?"

The elder smiled for the first time in months. "It might prove interesting."

"If you think an abundance of gold might cure the madness, I would like to meet with you in private session at a later time and presently request that not one word of this meeting's content escape the church."

"Your wishes are granted," said the elder. "Not one of us will speak of what has transpired here, and I will meet with you immediately after we sing together."

For the first time in many weeks, exuberant song filled the rafters and a fragile peace seemed to settle on the gathering.

CHAPTER THREE

The following morning the miner and his eldest son set out for the Red Mountain as was their custom and refused Oudeis permission to accompany them. He was outraged.

"You cannot deny me permission. I am the richest man in all of Harmony."

"It is not true. You only have the most gold and the most abundant possessions, but 'the ant is surfeited with a crust of bread.' Today my son and I want to be alone."

"I can travel by myself," said Oudeis haughtily.

"And you can be swallowed by the spring waters which have crested to their peak."

Oudeis knew the miner was right and angrily galloped off.

The miner and his eldest son took the accustomed route to the Red Mountain, then rode westward for almost a mile. Near the mouth of the Singing River they stopped when they approached an ancient eruption of dark rusted quartz on a long, narrow ridge. It was on the bank below the ridge that Oudeis had found his tiny nuggets and the flakes of gold.

The miner motioned to his son to bring the picks and he himself gathered up two large metal scuttles grown dark with the dust of iron ore and coal. They walked upstream to a familiar sandbar and waded chest-deep in turbulent water across the Singing River. Then they climbed to the top of the ridge and the miner began tapping with his pick.

"Is there gold here, father?"

"Yes. When I was a boy of your age, the blacksmith and I were digging here in search of coal deposits and found an entire rock of gold. Although it was beautiful it had no value to us at the time and we returned to Harmony only with our coal. A week or so ago we remembered our discovery and suddenly realized what it was."

He began chipping more vigorously with his pick and dislodged several pieces of quartz heavily laden with gold. He continued to attack the quartz until a large rock fell aside and there was a massive vein of the purest gold. It was the mother lode.

The boy gasped. "There must be wagonloads of gold!"

"Yes," said the miner. "Go back to the wagon, careful to cross at the sandbar. Otherwise the swollen river will devour you. Take the rope and tie one end to the oak tree nearest the wagon, then tie a piece of metal to the other end and hurl it across the stream to me."

The boy did as he was told, and soon the miner carefully guided scuttles full of gold across the Singing River to his son. The boy untied the rope and sent the empty scuttles back to the miner to again be filled with chunks of gold. A few hours after lunch he called to his father.

"There is no more room in the wagon."

The miner again carefully crossed the river, and together they took the wagonload of gold back to Harmony.

Early in the morning, the miner and the blacksmith brought the wagon filled with gold to the cobblestone courtyard in front of the blacksmith's shop. There they waited impatiently for the village to wake from sleep. Soon there were wisps of smoke rising from chimneys as the housewives prepared breakfast and the children stumbled out to feed the livestock. A half hour later the streets began to fill up with people. The cobbler walked by on his way to work. Once a friendly man, he now barely nodded as he passed. Suddenly, almost as an afterthought, he glanced at the wagon gleaming in the morning sunlight.

"What in the world?" He gasped. "Is that all . . . gold?" He could barely get out the words.

"Indeed," said the miner. "Would you like some?"

"You're joking!"

The miner never changed his expression and handed him two ten-pound nuggets.

"I can't believe it. . . . I . . . I . . ." He grasped the gold like a starving man clutches a loaf of bread and went staggering off down the street.

"Come back for more," said the blacksmith. "There's plenty for everyone!"

Soon a crowd had gathered, the miller and the mayor, the tanner and the woodsman, their wives and children as well, all shoving and screaming for the gold. By the time Oudeis heard of the miracle and saw huge nuggets of gold moving through the streets in every direction, there was hardly any left. The people who normally stepped aside as he rode by now ignored him. When the cobbler's wife shouted at him, "Now we're richer than you are, Oudeis," he jumped from his horse and fought his way through the mob. Unfortunately there were only a few small nuggets remaining in the bottom of the wagon, and Oudeis was on his hands and knees fighting with the healer's wife and children for his share of the gold.

"There will be more tomorrow," said the miner. And there was. Another wagonload. Many of the people had stayed up all night and waited at the blacksmith's courtyard. By the time the sun rose and the wagon reappeared, an angry, feverish mob had already assembled. The miner and the blacksmith began handing out nuggets to every hand that clawed pleadingly at the air. Clothes were ripped, hats trampled, and the tanner's wife was knocked unconscious when a large nugget fell on her head.

"Calm down," said the miner. "There's enough for everyone!"

But his words were to no avail. The roar of the crowd continued with Oudeis fighting frantically for the largest nugget until finally the last pennyweight was gone and people made their way home to assess what they had captured. Oudeis was furious. A hundred people in Harmony were now wealthier than he was. He fumed half the night and then made his way to the crowd that had assembled in darkness. They jeered at him.

"We'll build a house twice the size of yours, Oudeis!"

"And have a hundred more cattle!"

"And rings of solid gold for every finger!"

Oudeis said nothing and waited until the wagon reappeared. Then he fought his way to the front and grabbed two of the largest chunks of gold. As he forced his way back through the crowd someone tripped him and in an instant someone else had run away with his gold. When he fought his way to the front again, only the same small particles as before remained. He greedily gathered up what he could and disappeared, never noticing the sad eyes of the blacksmith's daughter, Raven, who remembered the Oudeis who had first made her a ring of gold.

As soon as he returned to his home, Oudeis decided to follow the miner's wagon from afar and learn the source of the mother lode. Then he could fill his own saddlebags with as much gold as they could carry. He packed a few pieces of bread and a miner's pick and was off at an excited gallop. In the distance he saw the wagon as it wound its way through the hills. He watched the miner and his son turn off at the road that led to the mouth of the Singing River and saw them cross at the sandbar and climb to the high ridge where the mother lode gleamed brighter than any star he had ever seen.

When the wagon was filled in midafternoon and the miner and his son departed, Oudeis made his way down a hill to the edge of the river at the sandbar. Gently he encouraged his horse into the stream and across the water. On the opposite bank the horse slipped on a rock and almost fell back into the tumultuous water. Then Oudeis was safe on the opposite shore and cautiously made his way to the top of the ridge. He approached the deep crevice of gold, now almost a cave, as a pilgrim approaches an ancient shrine. Then with a shout of triumphant joy, he began hacking away at the gold. Soon he had filled the large saddlebags with giant nuggets of gold until they could hold no more. With great effort he tied the bags on his horse and climbed on. The horse could hardly move and Oudeis knew that the beast could never make it across the hissing water. He climbed off and led the horse to the edge of the bank near the sandbar. Then Oudeis stepped into the water which was almost up to his shoulders, planted his feet cautiously, and led the horse down into the stream. It resisted, but finally under Oudeis' strong urging it stepped into the water. Slowly, almost reverently, Oudeis led the struggling animal across, careful to plant his own foot as he made each step in the raging current.

As he neared the bank, he began laughing almost hysterically. There was more gold in his saddlebags than anyone in Harmony possessed. Once again he would be the richest and most envied man in the village. Giddily he began climbing up the bank until he reached the top and let out an exhilarating scream of joy. Startled, the horse lurched dangerously and

slid back awkwardly into the water. Oudeis clung desperately to the reins and tried to pull the animal up the bank. Again the horse panicked and almost fell to its left side. Horror stricken, Oudeis watched the chunks of gold slide from the saddlebag into the stream. As the horse tried to steady itself, it tottered to its right and again the gold began to slide from its leather cache. Oudeis let go of the reins and lunged for the gold. He grabbed one giant nugget of approximately thirty pounds and fell with it into the stream. The horse, finally rid of the burden of gold, thrashed and fought its way up the bank, while Oudeis, still clutching the nugget, was washed down the Singing River and drowned in its depths with his gold.

Later that night, the horse returned to Harmony with the saddlebags still strapped on and a few particles of gold at the bottom. It was obvious to the whole village what had happened. Only the elders and the blacksmith's family felt any real grief. Only Raven shed tears.

CHAPTER FOUR

In the morning the wagon again appeared, loaded with gold. The rumor of Oudeis' disappearance and probable death now had circulated throughout the village, but had little impact on the unruly mob that fought for their ration of gold with the same shrill screams and passionate hunger, the same shoving and mauling that ignored the daffodils already blooming on the bank of the Singing River. Only a few like the blacksmith's family rejoiced in the fresh smells of spring's new life and the busy swallows rushing frantically to build their nests under the eaves of the colorful houses of Harmony. After the last scrap of gold had been scraped from the wagon, the miner and his son again set out to extract the precious metal from the mother lode. It was during lunch that they discovered the body of Oudeis rolling against a fallen log a hundred yards downstream from the sandbar crossing, his rigid arms frozen around the massive nugget. They lifted his body and carried it to the wagon.

It was on that same afternoon that a strange paralysis took possession of Harmony. The tanner went to the miller for fine flour and offered him a tiny nugget of gold which once would have purchased half a year's worth of flour.

"I have no need of gold," said the miller. "Half our woodbox is full of it. I need leather for my children's shoes and wood for my wife's stove."

The tanner was amazed. "But I have no leather or wood. Only gold."

It was the same everywhere. Suddenly gold was superfluous and the whole village was in an uproar. The butcher had a little meat but no flour or shoes, and the cobbler had a few pairs of sandals but no wood or meat.

"What good is our gold?" the people asked angrily.

The elders smiled. "What good indeed?"

When the wagon returned in the late afternoon and drove past the church, the whole village seemed to be gathered in the square.

"We have no need of your gold!" they shouted. "Bring us coal and iron. Our homes are cold and our wagons are in disrepair. Our children go hungry and even our horses are wasted and thin."

When the crowd noticed the body of Oudeis, there was a moment of stunned silence, then a scream of rage.

"He is the source of our trouble! Throw his body into the Singing River and let the fishes feast on his evil remains!"

As they rushed to the wagon to destroy the corpse of Oudeis, the most revered of the elders held them back with an upraised arm.

"Assemble in the church!" he said. "And ring the bells that everyone may come."

For the first time in weeks the pews were filled with people, frantic and angry. The elder addressed them.

"Do you have enough gold?" he asked.

"Yes!" they shouted in unison. "Gold is evil and the source of our destruction! It is a curse!"

"No," said the elder. "Gold is beautiful, fired in the depths of the

earth and cast upon the land for our enjoyment. It is God's creation but we have made of it a desecration. If it were necessary for our life and happiness, it would be as abundant as the water and the wheat, as available as the sky and the sun which warms our hearts and gives life to the earth. As beautiful as the gold is, it is nothing compared to a child's wondering eyes or the gentle, patient eyes of a cat or dog."

"Take our gold!" the crowd shouted. "We no longer have need of it. It buys nothing. Only the labor of our hands can bring life to our families! Oudeis has almost destroyed us."

"No, Oudeis has not done anything save expose the greed and hatred that can infect the human heart. He has done us a favor."

"What favor has he done?" the cobbler shouted angrily.

"He has tested us and we failed. Why did we not give him the finest house without his asking, the largest flock, and most ornate possessions? Then he would have learned from us that love and honest labor are the source of human joy and too many possessions are a burden that empties the heart and dries the spirit."

He paused. "Oudeis did not harm us. We failed him! His death is as much ours as it is his own. Tomorrow we will bury his body with dignity and sing our sadness to the heavens in his honor!"

"But what of the gold?" the mayor asked. "We must destroy it!"

"It cannot be destroyed," said the elder. "It is part of the earth. We will gather it all together and make a giant monument in the square to mark our own madness. Each family shall have a single drinking cup made of solid gold and once a year we shall all drink water from that cup. We shall recite the ancient proverb: 'It is not the beauty of the cup that matters, but the purity of its water; not the comeliness of a face, but the purity of its spirit.' "

"We have only learned what we already know! Now we must ask forgiveness of God and one another."

"But what of Oudeis' home? Should we tear it down stone by stone?" asked the mayor.

"No," said the elder. "We shall leave it as a place for the next stranger who arrives in our midst. We shall not force our way on him. He must learn it all by himself."

Even as the fledgling swallow must fall from the nest before he flies and the wolf cub must know the mouse from the poisonous adder.

Then the people of the whole village sang their traditional songs to the darkening skies and the crests of the Explorer Mountains. To the tall, shimmering pines and in harmony with the roar of the Singing River that made its way westward in the endless circle of life.

"I loved Oudeis," said Raven to her father on the way home.

"I know," he said, "but not all loves are possible. Some will destroy us, a true love will open our heart and give life to our whole being. It is from such love that you were born. Oudeis was not as fortunate as you."

"I will keep his ring," she said.

"As long as you like. It was perhaps his finest moment of love."

"Perhaps I did not love him enough?"

"No," the blacksmith said softly. "Love takes a long time. It is a gentle force like the river making smooth the rough edges of rocks or like the moss growing on the trunks of oaks. Love cannot invade like an avalanche in the mountains or the north wind which topples the cypress."

He paused thoughtfully. "Love is a rare gift like the gold that lurks quietly in quartz or the secret spring that bubbles from the depths of the earth. It is hard to love someone who does not share your deepest hopes and most secret dreams. Perhaps it is impossible. Even when love comes, it must be cherished, or it will wither and die."

"If I truly want love, will I finally find it?" she asked.

"I think so," he answered hesitantly. "But you must find someone who thinks you beautiful as you are. Even as I do! 'The gopher does not envy the mink's fur nor does the rabbit regret that he does not fly like the dove.'"

"How will I know when I find such love?"

"You will smell the lilacs and taste the sweetness of the air. You will notice the changes in the trees and hear the song of birds, you will embrace the snow and listen to the melody of the river. You will laugh from your legs and cry from your loins and embrace each new day as a gift that will never come again. Most of all you will greet the sun each morning with reverence and feel the joy and sadness of the sunset. And you will never lose the special beauty that is you. No one can ask that, nor will love permit it! This above all!"

The following Sunday in mid-April, as the people gathered in the church, there was again the evidence of tranquility that had forever characterized life in Harmony. Parents had again taken charge in their homes, and husbands and wives and children seemed content with their work. The miller was again delighted to make the finest flour and exchange with the cobbler and tailor for the best of their own craft. Song rang out more loudly than before and the most revered of the elders rose to recite the ancient story of the planting celebration.

Once a man was thirsting at the bottom of a high hill. His eyes saw the deer gathering at the brow of the hill to drink and his ears heard the splashing of water. At the bidding of his eyes and ears the man began to climb, but his feet objected: "Why must we obey the ears and eyes and work so hard? The knees do nothing!" So he began to walk on his knees. Soon the knees complained: "What of the hands?" Immediately he began walking on his hands, but the hands pointed out the futility of the climb since only the mouth wanted water. Finally the man collapsed and died on the hill. We, all of us, are that man and each part depends on the whole. No one is greater or less, no one is sufficient to himself. Thus says our ancient wisdom.

Then the church was filled with song that echoed beyond the Explorer Mountains until the whole village gathered in the public square to share bread and fruit. To celebrate once more the end of winter and the joy of spring and to watch the Singing River flow relentlessly toward the sea in an unending circle of life.

Finis